liyvan 970310@gmail.com

Father's Philosophy

SECOND EDITION

Linda

*

Poems by

Patrick T. Randolph

*

Introduction by

Vernon E. Johnson

POPCORN PRESS
PO BOX 12
Elkhorn, WI 53121

Cover design by Katheryn Smith & Stephen D. Sullivan
Photos by Darlene M. Randolph & Haluk Asna
Typesetting by Lester Smith

To my wife, Gamze, and her gentle care,
To my mother, Darlene, and Father, Gerald,
for being there,
To Ayfer and Haluk's silent smiling stare;

And special thanks to Kristi, Kelly, Erol, Doug,
Jim, Claudia and Vernon, Bobe and Ila,
Don, Lester, Cathy, Virginia, and John.

Table of Contents

❧ III: Cloud Curiousity ❧

❧ IV: The Reverence of Small Hands ❦

❧ V: May's Voice ❦

Acknowledgments

The author would like to extend a warm thanks to the editors of the following publications in which these poems, some in slightly different versions, have appeared:

Beginnings: "Zen Visit" (The title has changed to "Hummingbird's Hide and Seek Hello.")

Bellowing Ark: "Music and Bread," "Reverence of Small Hands," "Baiting the Hook," "An Apple on the Kitchen Table," "May Day Baskets," and "From Philosophers to Dragonflies"

Bell's Letters: "Your Hands: For the Child to Come," "An Ant, A Bee, God and Me," "Celebrating Trees," "Silent Genius," and "Heaven"

BlackWidows Web of Poetry: "Cloud Curiosity"

Brevities: "Consequence of Love"

ByLine Magazine: "My Uncle in Iowa"

California Quarterly: "The Recyclers"

The Discerning Poet: "In July," "Star," "Original Grin," and "The Quilter Creating"

The Door Peninsula Voice: "Father's Philosophy"

Free Verse: "Corn Planting Time," "Deer Lake Reflection," "Dusk on the Ridge," "Language of the Soil," and "Silhouette"

Museletter: "The Cheese God"

New Author's Journal: "Mother-Daughter Music"

Niigata Joho—An English Journal: "Sleep," "Bones," and "Unfolding"

Northern Stars Magazine: "Paddle's Soul"

Oak: "Star" and "Finger Kiss"

Offerings Quarterly: "Splitting Firewood"

The Pink Chameleon: "Taking Advantage of My Free Time"

Poetry Depth Quarterly: "The Blossom" (Also reprinted in *Storyteller*.)

Poetry Haven: "Love Is Here"

Poetry Motel: "Without Stopping"

Poetry Soup: "The Grinning Truth"

Rearview Quarterly: "American Dream in November"

The Rockford Review: "A Bar in Berkeley," "Me-ing and You-ing," "Sundays with Favre" and "My Wife Returning From Turkey"

The Rockford River Times: "Human Economics," "Soul-Editing," "February Dance," and "My Nose Considering Your Nose"

Sensations Magazine: "Words Melt Like Snow"

TMP Irregular: "From the Car Window on the Passenger's Side"

Toyosaka Koho: "Snowflake Philosophy" (Originally written and published as a haiku.)

TrailBlazer Magazine: "Just Up the Road—Early May"

Wisconsin Poets' Calendar 2002: "Barefoot in the Sand"

Wisconsin Poets' Calendar 2005: "Turtle Euphoria"

Wisconsin Poets' Calendar 2010: "A Wind God"

Write On!!: "Weeding the Salad Garden," "Because You Are Beans," "My Wife's Hum," "Flight to Full Moon," "Trees and Snow," "Grandma Kohlbusch's Voice," "The Poet," "Song of My Eyelashes," and "Winter's Laughter"

Anthologies

Colors of Life: "Festival of Moon and I"

Treasured Poems of America: "Because You Are Beans"

Voices Anthology: "Snowflake Philosophy"

Awards

"Words Melt Like Snow" was selected as a winner for the 2004 Louise Messer Memorial Contest sponsored by *Oak Magazine,* and as a winner for the Annual Winter Poetry Contest sponsored by *Sensations Magazine.* "Baiting the Hook" received an honorable mention for the 2005 Rockford Writers' Guild Ides of March Contest. "Celebrating Trees" was selected for the Malaschak-Clubb Award from *Bell's Letters.*

Special Thanks

I would like to thank the editors of Popcorn Press, Vernon E. Johnson, and my father, Gerald R. Randolph, for their time and helpful insights in editing this manuscript. I would also like to deeply thank my mother, Darlene, for her constructive criticisms. And I am forever grateful to my wife, Gamze. Her support and cheerful smile throughout the various stages of developing this collection are appreciated beyond what words could ever express. Her gentle care is precious.

An Introduction

In an urban-centered, technological society, where industrial concrete steadily advances while grass and trees become rarities consigned to the occasional public park, Patrick T. Randolph, thanks to extraordinary parents, had the opportunity to grow up in a remote Eden in the woods of northern Wisconsin, in an atmosphere that combined intellectual achievement with the practical challenges of survival, year after year. Like Thoreau, his father and mother, refugees from academe, built their own cabin on a lake and read to him at night after performing such tasks as harvesting wild rice with the local Indians during the day. So Patrick grew up listening to Shakespeare as well as the howling northern winds.

Like many solid poets, Patrick is well traveled as well as widely read. His major literary influences include (naturally) the English Romantics, especially Keats; American poets from Dickinson to Sexton; and the distinguished writers of Japan, Spain, and Turkey, countries in which he has spent much of his adult life. Especially significant in this last group are Nazim Hikmet, the great modern Turkish poet, along with the much earlier Rumi and Emre; Garcia Lorca, Machado, and Jiminez of Spain; and Ryokan of Japan, the Zen monk who fell in love with a young nun when he was 70 years of age. Patrick has also learned to speak and write the languages of the places in which he has lived.

Readers of Patrick's poems will find here succinct vignettes of the people that have formed his life: his wife anticipating the cold whiteness of snow which she knows is indispensable to the warm redness of summer's harvest; an Iowa uncle perpetuating himself in autobiographical stories; a wise father calmly sending the young boy off to repair a window he has broken, instead of punishing him; his mother bringing coffee and good cheer to men planting corn; both parents as harmonious melodies of a single song, like the ones they listen to in kneading good energy into good bread. Literarily, there is the character of the adult Jesus bringing to his final vision a memory of trees, flowers, grass, and wild things of his childhood, all lifting him up to a higher view of a complex world.

Patrick, a scholar of philosophy, freely mixes ideas and subtle nuances of life with pictures of nature. The natural world of a remote lake house in northern Wisconsin is more rugged than the one seen from a cottage at Grasmere, but the love of nature in all its aspects is innately still there.

The thoughts that emerge from Patrick's poems, while springing from many sources, are surprisingly in accord with that of our Transcendental ancestors, who would have nodded in sure approval of his childhood.

Essentially a mystic like Henry David Thoreau and Ralph Waldo Emerson, and having been instructed in both Christianity and Buddhism, Patrick is nurtured, inspired, and absorbed by the spirit that resides in nature. Like Emerson, Patrick senses that to know God one must know oneself and study nature.

Like Thoreau tracing his spiritual growth and renewal, Patrick's poetry mirrors the cycle of nature from spring planting to November dreams of summer.

Throughout the poetry there are moments when, in losing the self in the spirit of nature, the poet transcends the material world, as Emerson wrote in *Nature*:

In the woods, we return to reason and faith...the currents of the Universal Being circulate through me; I am part or parcel of God.

The most succinct statement of the Transcendental moment in Patrick's poetry comes in "May's Voice," a pattern poem that speaks of falling to Earth before rising to "infinity."

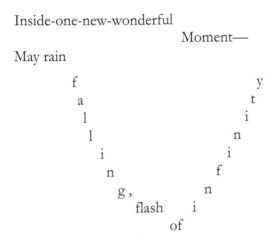

Inside-one-new-wonderful
                              Moment—
May rain

          f   y
        a   t
        l   i
         l   n
          i   i
           n   f
          g,   n
            flash   i
                of

Transcendence and regeneration are compelling themes throughout Patrick's poetry, "Baiting the Hook" being one of the strongest examples.

One is reminded of Thoreau, measuring a pond that reflects the stars and deciding that "Heaven is under our feet as well as over our heads," and that "The pure Walden water is mingled with the sacred water of the Ganges." In Patrick's "Baiting the Hook," the uplifting moment comes as he waits and waits and waits—also on a body of renewing water—for a fish to take his bait:

The joy of emptying all from the mind,
The self-realization of being born and born again.

Readers of these poems will find themselves thrust into the great essence of the moment and asked to reflect on the intricacies of nature and the carefully crafted imagery which unfolds with each line of Patrick's verse. To be sure, this collection of poems is a journey of sorts—one that will, in fact, cheerfully linger in the mind long after the poems have been read.

—Vernon E. Johnson

❧ I ❧

Sipping Laughter

Sipping Laughter

May Moon—
         Ancient woman,
         Newborn child,
Sipping Laughter
         From the cups
         Of my eyes.

Love Is Here

Love unbuttons
Its coat,
Takes off Its shoes,
Puts Its hat
On the rack,
And walks into the living room
And every room
With a soft summer autumn winter spring song
Singing
From every and all imaginable
Pores
Of Its amazing body, soul, spirit
And overwhelming
Mind!

Love shouts and shouts in tickling
Intoxicating
Silence,

"Stand up, live, be and embrace
The meaning of all that matters!"

Love is here and has no intention
Of leaving,

And why leave when Love's life begins
With each moment of
Every moment's now?

Unfolding

I use a piece
                of laughter
To open up—
                your lips.

Festival of Moon and I

From the Moon's outstretched arms,
Her fingertips
Sing out like roses desiring
The attention of human touch.

From my eyes' outstretched hands,
These fingertips
Are small hearts grinning great grins,
And celebrating this

Late autumn festival
Of Moon's desire to touch
My eyes' small hearts embracing

The unforgettable newness
Of an unimaginable
Unmistakable
Us!

Old Ladies, Night Insects

Night insects
Converse like a band of old ladies.

I listen through the open window—

Chatter-crackle-chirp,
Chirp-chatter-crackle,
Crackle-chatter-chirp!

I understand nothing
Other than they like to hear themselves
Toss their voices into the night—

Old ladies doing verbal somersaults:
Exercising their undulating quality of sound,
Perfecting their ability to sing without singing.

Yes, these insects have enthusiastic teeth and tongues.

Night insects,
Old ladies,
Sans the sound of teacups clinking—

Chatter-crackle-chirp,
Chirp-chatter-crackle,
Crackle-chatter-chirp!

The remarkable thing is
I do believe
They are saying
Something wise!

Baiting the Hook

I bait the hook with a plump red worm
I caught this morning roaming in our asparagus patch.
Looking at this delicious meaty phenomenon,
I can imagine the pleasure felt by the fish
Upon discovering it in the cool clear water.

I finish baiting the hook,
Cast my line in the late afternoon lake,
And then I wait.
I wait.

Waiting is the essence of fishing,
Eliciting the mysticism of the act,
The heart of Eros,
The anticipation of what might be and become,
The joy of emptying all from the mind,
The self-realization of being born and born again
With every moment while
The wait, the great wait goes on:

The wait,
The perfect wait,
The grinning wait,
The omnific wait,
The wait.

For when the fish hits the hook and takes the bait,
The magic of imagination is gone:
The erotic pulse,
The mystic nothingness,
The ideal dreams of compassion,
The joy of emptying all from the mind
Is replaced

By the sudden duty of catching the fish,
Reeling it in with patient motion,
Bringing it to the dock
And praying to the god of fish—promising
That I will accept full responsibility for
Taking the fish's life
For the sake of my own.

Me-ing and You-ing

I am the me of Me-ing
And
You are the you of You-ing!

So let us celebrate inside our every moment's
Joy, our every moment's Birth

Of this magnificent Me-ing,
Of this miracle You-ing
                    In Every-thing that is,
                    In Every-where that is,
                    In Every-time that is

Now while it nurtures
The creative creativity
Of a forever New
Yet well polished Old

Me-ing and You-ing

That lives, works, and breathes in clear lemon
Candy colored transparency mixed with a blueberry smile,

As we grow—growing in synchronicity,
And ripen—ripening with serendipity
Into magical fruit bigger than any laugh
Of Infinity's Soul.

Yes, let us go, then, Me-ing and You-ing
With the rhyme of Do-ing and New-ing

In our mosaic of many and one,

In our web of one and many's

Perfect separate
Togetherness.

Yes, oh yes, let us go, then,
                    Me-ing and You-ing—
And plunge soakingly into
                    Everything born
                    Inside this
                    Absolutely sweet

Moment's now of our
Bellowing, Beautiful, and Blithe birth!

Yes, oh, yes!

Let us go, then,
                    You-ing and Me-ing,
Let us be, then,
                    Me-ing and You-ing—

As you are the you of You-ing
Constantly making you a newer transcended You,
And I am the I of I am making me a
More remarkable Me.

Yes, oh, yes—

You are the you of You-ing
And I
I am the me of Me-ing!

Your Hands: For the Child to Come

Because of your new hands
On my old hands

And the feel
Of their humorous human
Miracle of warm giggles,

My heart's voice
Has learned
With all its celebration
Of bird intoxicating songs,

That there is no better
Vocation than singing
To any and everything

That is!

Self-Love

The ears of two words in a philosophy text
Find themselves laughing
At each
Other

Unable
To stop—

Expression
            of Self-Love.

Human Economics

A homeless man on the street selling
Newspapers,

His pockets bulging with more life
Than my own.

We look at each other, nod and exchange smiles:
Each of us understanding, knowing and accepting
Responsibility for the other's emotional well-being

Of being well and being kind:

Kind to our grins,
Kind to our eyes,
Kind to our moment together—

Passing each other's
Transparent miracle,
Here—on this shadowed South-Side street.

Overcast Skies, Summer Wind

I catch a small body of wind
In my cupped hands,

And hold it as a child holds
The tiny body of a firefly.

The wind's voice echoes—
Fluttering against my skin.

I open my hands and let my invisible firefly
Escape in all directions

With endless euphoria,

Moving about like a small conductor
Performing his final curtain call.

Patrick T. Randolph

Barefoot in the Sand

being a being
of Being
with beings
being beings,
and being
a being in and out
of becoming,
but always
being
a being
of Being
being
in love
and in life
with beings,
I think it is good
to walk barefoot
                in the sand.

Without Stopping

Traveling on the 8:05 Duluth bound
Evening bus,

Again

I find the *Greyhound* driver tapping
His solid plump red fingers
On the steering wheel,

Keeping time
To the music in his head.

There are moments I can hear his song,
Feel his thoughts,
Understand his voice.

The driver and I stare searchingly at the centerline.

The centerline—
Soundless and strong
Does not lie.

True to its accepting curves, yellow guidance, and
Determined path,

The centerline goes on and on—
Faithfully

Without stopping.

Small Change

God stopped by
A church
The other day,

It stayed long
Enough
For *Her* to feel
Each member
Of the congregation
Feel *His*
Presence,

And then
It scooted up the street,
Filled with hot sun
And cool shadows,
To stand outside a small
Coffee shop
As a sad manifestation
Of a homeless woman
Happily wearing
Her old lover's
Oversized
Raincoat
With the hood pulled over
His face,
So you could only hear
Her voice
As *It* asked
For
Small change.

Flight to Full Moon

Full Moon is giving
Birth to countless grinning eyes
Opening wider—

While clear winged souls from bodies
Return to Her round white womb!

❧ II ❦

Father's Philosophy

Father's Philosophy

My father, while I was growing up,
Never hit me, not ever,
Not even for the most foolish things I'd done.

Once, when I was pitching an imaginary no-hitter
In front of our house, I lost control
Of the baseball

And struck the kitchen window out— clean out;
A perfect series of pitches topped with a shattering finish.

No cheers from the crowd in the tall green, white pine
    bleachers;
But Dad came running from the garden behind the house.

He stood there assessing the aftermath of my pitch.
My glove suddenly weighed more than the Earth I was
    standing on.
I stood staring at the window, hoping it would pick
Itself up and return to the dugout.

Dad looked at me like a coach deciding whether or not
To take his star pitcher out of the game.

This short silence was longer than the entire history
Of the World Series.

Finally, he said,
"You know where the tools are,
And I've taught you once how to repair windows.
Best get to work. Your mother likes looking out
That window, and I'm partial to it myself."

He walked away, disappearing
Into the tomato patch.
I walked off the pitcher's mound
And into the garage.

Corn Planting Time

for Mom

It's corn planting time in northern Wisconsin.
Dad and I have waited for the perfect Spring sprinkle;
Not a strong rain that washes soil and insects away
In the night, but a long, long soaking rain,
One that will prepare the soil for our fingers while they push
The tiny seeds of corn with ease into the sweet, black, musty
    smelling earth,

A long, loquacious, soft sprinkle that will call earthworms
Out to play with our odd, human, worm-like fingers that peck
In and out of the soil like a neurotic bird not sure of
What he is looking for, or what he will find.

The rain continues all day even after we have broken
For a short lunch and returned to the green festival of planting
    corn.

A robin watches from a nearby fence post
With wanderlust eyes bathing in the Spring sprinkle.

Mom is coming down the driveway
With a thermos of hot coffee in one hand,
And a wave in the other.

From the Car Window on the Passenger's Side

Passing a small town in the middle
Of a Wisconsin cornfield:

One old woman is sweeping her front steps,

A dog chases his tail while waiting
For his children to come home from school.

A gray-bearded man with a yellow baseball cap
Enters a bar he calls a cafe—
His coat torn and patched with duct tape.

And the grocery store on the corner
Of nowhere and maybe somewhere

Covers its windows with discount signs
To hide how bare it is inside.

Patrick T. Randolph

My Uncle in Iowa

Morning coffee;

Sunlight on your arms,
You squint and take a drink,

Listening to me
Tell a story
About my uncle in Iowa
I recalled just now when
The wind made

The white kitchen curtains move
Like the walking-waving arms

Of an animated old man
In the middle of one of his afternoon tales:

Hitchhiking to New Orleans,
Summer of the stolen car,
Starting out as a barber in Des Moines,
Or the comedy of pouring cement.

Beer on his lips and words pouring forth
From each hand's loquacious finger
Darting in the air—

Telling stories, old stories alive
With the magic of then,

Tales continually
Here inside my ear— echoing
My uncle's voice in Iowa.

Music and Bread

Mother and Father
Are making bread in the kitchen.

Sometimes they laugh, sometimes
They are serious and silent, and sometimes
They pinch each other and play,

But they always listen to music
While making bread.

"You need good energy and good music
To make good bread.
It all goes into the dough,
Making the bread what it is," says Pops.

"You need good energy and good music
Otherwise there is no body, no taste;
The bread will not have anything to say,
And it will not grin or sing.
The bread will not be alive and grow,
Or have the power to do even the simplest thing."

Good music, good bread.

Mother and Father— sometimes serious, silent,
Sometimes playing, giggling,
But always listening, listening to music,

To good music

While making bread
In the early afternoon kitchen.

Mother-Daughter Music

for Haluk and Ayfer

Now the amazing magic of music starts,
A mother's teasing fingers on the pink bare
Skin of her daughter's tiny toes.

First the touch, then the giggle—
Silence creating sound.
The daughter's giggle is contagious,
Intoxicating—
Her mother joins in, waves of laughter
Rushing cheerfully about the room,
Undulating
Like the pounding of the Summer sea.

Her father has just come up the stairs and stops:
Standing behind the closed door of his daughter's room,
Stopping to listen to the giggling
Girls—this mother-daughter music.

He refrains from laughing,
He refrains from opening the door and dancing in,
He refrains from clapping for this great overture,
This mother-daughter sound,
This poetry of voices,
This soul-soaring experience of vocal affection.

His shadow on the door disappears and enters his bedroom—
The melody of his own soft whistle commanding his lips.
He prepares the bed for his wife: the genuine, the irreplaceable,
The endless musician of infectious love.

The Recyclers

We are all natural recyclers
Of the most avid kind.
The concept is not new,
It did not start
With secondhand chewed
Gum shared by your first love
In the fourth grade,
Not with the hand-me-downs
From Uncle Bobe,
Or the Goodwill store
On the corner of Ninth
And Washington,
Not with the saving of tin foil
During the Second World War.
No, recycling started with the re-
Using of souls—
From the time when we first were
To the time when it will be
Absolutely incomprehensible
To know just how many faces
And voices
Our souls have used
As meek and mighty masks.

Patrick T. Randolph

In July

Cool blue night dew
On our shiny bare white feet,
Star history in our eyes—

We walk the Wisconsin
Summer fields; our ears collecting
Cricket voices in the dark.

Paddle's Soul

for Dad

My wooden paddle draws
Circles in the dark lake water
That crash whisperingly against
The old fiberglass canoe.

My paddle never tires
Of this motion as it learns
The power of my hands' grip,
The dance of my arms' swing.

It dips into the evening's
Shadowed water then flies out
Into the air, dripping water circles
In perfect lines,

And listening to the itchy buzz
Of mosquitoes while it feels
The almost nonexistent landing legs
Of a curious dragonfly.

May Day Baskets

I recall the smell of orange gumdrops,
Spring's sweet morning fragrance— purple lilacs.
These, yes, these were the days of yellow tops,
Colorful ribbons, and other knickknacks
Found at my father's office door on May
Day, 1969. My father looked
Down at the basket, his eyes danced my way,
But my attention was already hooked
On the orange spice drops and tiny toys.
I stood by my father's long legs—delight
And joy tickled me as they do all boys
On the verge of discovering the sight
Of May Day baskets placed by Spring's fresh door,
So my legs flew forth, ascending the floor!

Splitting Firewood

Splitting oak logs—
I create halves with my axe
And watch these soulmates

Appear and fall on the snow;
They emit the raw bitter-sweet
Smell of loneliness.

I watch the split pieces lying
On the ground, faces up, hearts exposed,
And wondering

If they will be
Placed next to each other
On the woodpile near the house.

Patrick T. Randolph

Hummingbird's Hide and Seek Hello

The hummingbird is back—

Darting with green energy around the sweet cedar tree,
Playing hide and seek with my eyes,
Flirting with my curiosity,
Drinking her red wine from the feeder,

Singing at the top of her wings,
And saying hello at the window

Before
     Dis-
          Appearing
               Without a trace.

The Blossom

Returning home from school,
I enter an empty house.

Outside, in April's backyard,
I observe my mother and father

Holding hands, their gray hair—
Small kites in the wind.

They are bending over to look
At a new flower blossom in Mother's garden.

Its orange color as warm
As the sun on its velvet petals to be.

The zinnias she planted
Late last month have just begun

To point their color
In the direction of Apollo's grin.

I watch, I see,
I understand.

Today I returned home from school
And entered an empty house.

Now I stand at the open kitchen window
Learning another meaning of love,

Smiling at two gray kites in the backyard and their
Admiration for this flower blossom staring

Back into the wisdom
Of their early evening eyes.

Observing My Mother and Father's Morning Ritual of Love

To jump out of bed—

> To sing at the cool cat-tongued rigid
> Softness of the morning's breeze,
> As it stirs all living things into the spell
> Of welcoming life with a yawn!

To grin like the Autumn Moon larger than the sky—

> And yell at the top of my spirit's
> Miracle of musical
> Sound—"I love the You of You
> While your You-ing you becomes
> More of You than the you of yesterday!"

To kiss without stopping the You of You—

> While your You-ing you becomes
> More of You and Me than
> The We of Us of yesterday
> And all days of our morning Bliss!

To start each day's day

> Always
>> This way
>>> Without failing

To understand We are life's reason

> To celebrate love:
> To jump, to sing,
> To grin, to yell,
> To kiss, to hug

The passion for infinity

> And the affinity for everything
> That utters the celebration
> Of all that could possibly be
> And most commonly is!

❧ III ❧

Cloud Curiosity

Cloud Curiosity

A cloud presses

Her soft misty ear
To the ground,

Listening to earthworms
Dream of rain.

Patrick T. Randolph

Turtle Euphoria

A turtle's calm shell
—Wet from the Autumn night dew—
Reflecting star songs.

Winter's Laughter

Winter's laughter tickles leaves' fallen souls,
Making them dance inside this frigid hour.
Winter's laughter sips rain wine from these holes
On Earth, these puddles from a night shower.
Winter's laughter drunk with euphoric love,
Stumbles about the naked bare branched oaks,
Laughing louder and praising stars above.
Winter's laughter mixes with city folks,
Shows them how to dance morning, noon, and night,
Showing how to accept life with more life.
Winter's laughter now holds homeless men tight,
Embracing their spirits, cleansing their strife.
Yes, Winter's laughter is the Wind's proud song,
Loving Earth's warm breath and doing no wrong!

Star

Night after living Night—

One

Concentrated collection
Of Voices,

Sending a visual Song
                    to Earth.

Grandma Kohlbusch's Voice

Cleaning Grandma Kohlbusch's headstone,
I am assisted by Winter's restless winds,
By its long slender see-through
Fingers brushing away
The soul-less grass, the carcass of an ant,
Last Summer's oddly loquacious leaves.

Her name engraved in the stone becomes clear:
Rising up into the living vision of my eyes,
And the day she died sings now singing
Of birth's nervous excitement—

With a voice peaceful and rare.

Celebrating Trees

The weather forecast called for snow.
No snow arrived.

Now early February winds howl outside,
And play like scabby-kneed school children
In the trees.

They play without breaking for lunch.
They take no snacks, not even short wind naps.
These February winds play into the night.

And the trees, the trees speak sonnets—
Celebrating life with waving branches dancing,
Their wind enhanced voices shouting with
Intoxicated joy at my living room window.

I can no longer see the trees,
But hear their spirit tingling festival in the dark.

It excites me! It soaks me! It strengthens me!
It infects me! It teases me! It stimulates me!

Making my flesh, bones, and blood
Fully aware and alive—

They too now rock
With tree spirit
In the wind.

The Poet

The poet does not write,
Does not create.

The poet listens.

No act is more honorable, more beautiful,
More responsible,
More committed to life than listening.

The poet listens.

Yes, the poet listens
Until every bodily organ becomes
The miracle of the ear,
And every ear becomes an eye and every eye
Becomes the overwhelming
Power of love
While the eyes' vision listens—
And listening, yes—

This listening is the poet's self-less charm.

The strength of the poet's soul is listening
And listening the poet listens—

Listening,
Listening—

The poet *is* listening.

A Bar in Berkeley

Sunday afternoon bar,

The fresh crack of pool sticks in the dark corner, the piercing
    clink of glasses, the cackle
Of a middle-aged woman's laugh, laughing at something she
    finds funny because there is
Nothing else to do; she looks around, but no one is watching
    her.

Sunday afternoon bar,

An old man with long, oily hair and a nicely trimmed beard in
    leather biker clothes, who
Has never owned a bike, sits alone amused by a hockey game
    on TV. Some days he dunks
His pretzels in beer, but not today; today he just drinks and
    drinking he thinks.

Sunday afternoon bar,

The bartender looks at his watch then out the window beyond
    the *Miller Beer* sign, two
More customers waltz in, the hockey game goes on, the old
    man's fingers hold his cold
Glass of beer, the middle-aged woman has now turned 80 but
    still laughs as if she were 16.

Sunday afternoon bar.

Silent Genius

A CEO keeps a copy of the *New Testament*
In his desk,

But in the five years of acting
As head of the company,
Never
Once
Figured out
How

To open
        His drawers.

Window Opening

I've found again that window open
And now it opens, opening wider and surer
With the shy sexy winks coming from
The voice of my spirit's whispering song.

Ah, this window of my soul is open again
And again it calls, calling all light to gather
Together to form a love brighter than every
Laughing Moon's giggling face

In this, that or any
Imagined universe.

Ah, this window of my soul is open again
And again it calls, calling all light to gather
Together and show that it's all right to soak me
With the vivacious excitement of a child's desire

To enter all stages of life without
The slightest shadow of adult-fashioned fear.

Jesus as a Child

Jesus, as a child, loved
To play
With spiders and dragonflies,
With snakes and grasshoppers,
With bees and ladybugs.

He loved to talk to trees,
Ferns and flowers,
To the dew on grass
In red poppy-spotted fields.

He loved to listen to lakes, rivers,
Ponds and puddles tell
Stories of fish tickles
And Moon kisses,
But his favorite stories
Were told by frogs.

Jesus, as a child, grew up
And up and up and up—

Growing

He grew high, high, so high

Until he could see the World
Clearly
And perfectly
Through his adult eyes
With child-vision
From the cold, heat soaked cross.

Jesus's Eyes

Each one of Christ's eyes
On the cross spoke Compassion,

And winked winkingly wide with
Stinging sky blue stares

At a fly suddenly peeking
Lovingly inside

This soundless blue
Song of Nirvana.

February Dance

Dancing, I dance with the Wind despite
Her cold breasts and hips,
Her freezing fingertips.

She dances to feel the freedom
Of being human,

I dance to lose myself in the motion
Of Her arms.

She dances to grow-growing and love-loving
Every moment of our miracle fun
Here on this road of hard packed snow
And occasional patches of frozen dirt.

There are no trees on
This open country field.

I dance, We dance.
Oh yes, We dance
Because the Wind and Her voice's emotion
Need a partner to hold—
And I, I need to feel Her endless
Desire to grow-growing and love-loving
This wonderfully wild Wind-human waltz!

Life With Death

I

Death's powerful hands
Grabbed me at Birth shouting, "You
Are now *my* play thing!"

II

And befriending Death,
She took my pulse and counted
The beats of passion.

III

And discovering
Death's domain of aging time,
I sat with Her light.

IV

And growing up, I
Fell in love with Death's soft hands
And I felt Her soul.

V

And living with Death,
I shared Her desires and She
Listened to my fears.

VI

And looking into
Death's eyes with understanding,
I smiled forever.

VII

And entering Death's
Secrets with a schoolboy's grin,
I held Her small hands.

VIII

And feeling, I asked
If Death is an illusion—
And She winked with Love.

IX

And loving Death, I
Let Her into my soul
While She kissed my heart.

X

Now, as I lie here
Dying, Death whispers Her truth
And We part—for Good.

❧ IV ❧

The Reverence of Small Hands

The Reverence of Small Hands

A rock, untouched for decades by the sun, is pulled
Out of the earth by the small fingers of a boy's
Innocent love for plain, simple, magic looking rocks.

The rock is carried home in the boy's hands,
Juggled between both palms small and kind,
And then, prize-like, put carefully in his pocket
Next to another rock found earlier this morning.

The two rocks open their eyes to each other
In the dark moving pocket and whisper
A greeting of stone sound-full-less-ness,
Soundless sound understood only by rock souls.

They laugh and whisper, they grin and rejoice,
They bounce with the jump, run, trot of the boy's
Elated seven-year-old stride, they speak of earthworm
Songs during the dance of spring and summer rain,
The pounding of autumn lightning, the pecking of birds,
The warmth of a tree root, and the silver chill
Of the first frost of the year.

Then, arriving home, they join a large family of rocks
On the wooden writing desk in the boy's room.
The two rocks stare each other—spirits in love.

To them God has no meaning, their reverence for life
Is found in the small hands of a boy's grinning curiosity,
And his passion for collecting the magic joy of stones
On the surface of the earth and under the mystery of the soil.

Patrick T. Randolph

Trees and Snow

Trees
Watch the Snow fall—
Falling

Until the eyes and bodies of the Trees
Are all covered
With Snow,

Giant white
Gentle
Beings;

And these descending snowflakes
Watch—
Observing
The Trees—

Silence in love with Silence.

Room 112 for 3 Nights in D.C.

A motel room
Too big for just one person,

He turns
The TV on to fill up
This empty space;

The synthetic sound echoes—

Echoing
Off
The shy green walls.

Patrick T. Randolph

Park in January

No flowers in bloom, Winter trees
Speak in inward silence.

Snowflakes keep their mouths closed—
Concentrating on flight.

Words tossed around by a homeless
Man on a metal bench

Are consumed cravingly
By the Wind.

Words Melt Like Snow

for Cathy

My words seem to melt like snow before touching the ground,
The students sit in front of me pretending to listen.
But I swear all their left ears facing the window are really large
Bulging eyes staring at the first snowfall of the year.

My directions for the next assignment are coming to a close,
It is two minutes before recess and the looks on their faces
Exhibit an uncontrollable urge to run outside and make
Angels flying in the snow, to form that first snowball of the year,
To laugh at the top of their lungs and throw their arms open
Toward the white world of giggling snowflakes coming from
Above—tossed down by a generous cloud unknown.

I have finished now and a funny smile of relief falls into
My lips and soaks my face while I dismiss these little balls
Of anticipation out into a chorus of spontaneous grins—
Chasing after their own precious snowflake!

Bones

If my bones
            could see the Moon,
Would they
            grow taller?

Song of My Eyelashes

This dark room's song—
Waking up in the middle of the night
For a glass of cold water,

I listen to the music
Of my eyelashes beating against
Each other's feathered body

While I focus on the wise mirror
Reflecting a dream—
From across the shadowed room.

Patrick T. Randolph

Soul Editing

for John Wyatt

We all edit our psyche's verse,
The rhythm in the history of our souls—

Trying, yes, trying to become—
And be with Being—the perfect living poem.

Sun Swims

The Sun
Swims—
Swimming on the lake,

Then peeks into this blue
Wet transparent body
And whispers to fish:

Whispering love things and things of love,
Whispering rainbow colored words.

A young fish jumps
Out of the warm water—
Greeting evening's air;

The Sun rides—riding
Gently on a fish's
Scale.

New-ing

I am New
And will always be New and Newer by New-ing
With a Newness which is Newer than anything ever before.

I am New
And always have been ever since my Newness has been
(Re)newed by a Newer Me.

And this New New-ing Newness,
This forever New-ing inside each moment's now
Is God being God inside me being me.

Yes, this continual Renewing Newness
Is the reason I am New and New-ing and will always be
A New New-ing Newer (without ever being the Newest) Me.

The Grinning Truth

Saying it— the truth,

      it leaves my lips—

      the truth,

      and enters your ears—

      the truth,

      making you feel—

      the truth,

      making me free—

      the truth,

      making you see—

      the truth,

      making you touch—

      the truth,

      creating silence with sound—

      the truth,

      making you taste—

      the truth,

      making me grin—

      the truth.

Patrick T. Randolph

From Philosophers to Dragonflies

Plato wrote riveting haiku, but never told a single soul,
Socrates wrote tanka, but only in drunken states of joy,
And Aristotle composed renga, but never wrote them down.

Unfortunately, the only reliable recordings we have
Of these facts are in the souls of Plato, Socrates, and Aristotle—
But you see, they have all been reincarnated as dragonflies

Now diving and darting among the symphonic buzz
Of mosquitoes on this early Midwest evening so very far away
From their Greek home of ideal bodies and perfect minds.

The Cheese God

A thin northern Wisconsin fly finds a piece of warm cheese:
Lands on it, winks on it,
Grins on it,
And puts his fragile, feather-like hands together in a grand

Ritual of prayer and prays to his All Powerful,
Benevolent,
Omniscient, and always
Blissfully beaming

god of Cheese.

An Ant, A Bee, God and Me

Seeing an ant work-working in the hot summer sugar sand,
Observing a bee labor-laboring under the cool green of a shade
    tree,

I realize-realizing
The statement
"I am God"

Is the humblest,
Most sensitive and sensible,
The absolute truest set of three words

A living soul could ever utter and utter with confident sincerity.
"I am God," "I am God," "I am God" sings the ant, sings the
    bee, sings me!

Frog Farts—Voice of Spring

A newborn frog with new arms and legs
Emerges from the water.

This newborn frog farts out
A newborn song.

Surprised at such a hideous croaking sound
With hilarious notes,

He plops— plopping back in
With embarrassed skin,

Plopping into this grateful yet giggling
Plopped in, plopping pond.

Taking Advantage of My Free Time

I stand and wait;
I wait for the water to boil,
Then unwrap the package of noodles.

So many things to do this evening, now is a prime opportunity
To seize the moment and take advantage of the time.

I look at the broom in the corner, the dustpan, the pile of
Papers on my desk—projects everywhere of unfinished work.

I grin an elated grin, grinning with intentions of sweeping
The kitchen floor. Then I suck in the deepest breath my lungs will
    allow.

I watch an ant manipulate a crumb of sweet biscuit,
And carry it across the wooden, sun-warmed floor.

I grin again and release my breath. I watch and forget, forgetting
    all else
But the larger than life courage and astonishing effort

Of this tiny ant, the infinity of his will
And the agility of his
Small dancing feet.

❧ V ❧

May's Voice

May's Voice

Inside-one-new-wonderful

                              Moment—

May rain

```
        f                                    y
       a                                      t
       l                                      i
        l                                n
         i                               i
          n                            f
           g ,                      n
              flash          i
                       of
```

Patrick T. Randolph

A Bird's Philosophy

Listening to the Wind's voice,
Feeling the Wind's breath,
Understanding the Wind's whisper,
Embracing the Wind's soul;

Bird wings become the Wind's words—
Singing simple Sky songs.

Finger Kiss

What color
Do our fingers see

When they close
Their eyes and kiss—

Swinging between
You and me

On this Saturday
In the park?

Patrick T. Randolph

Heaven

Lucky humans experience
Heaven before
Earth;

It's Mother's miracle
Womb before
Birth!

American Dream in November

My wife looks forward to
The warm grasshopper-dancing
Summer day when we will

Harvest our first
Ripe red tomato from
The garden out back.

We look at each other this morning
On our walk, smelling the moist chance of
Snow on the damp, early winter wind.

Patrick T. Randolph

Original Grin

for Gamze

My soul's face—
slowly changing
                    after all these years—
back
        to
            its
                original grin.

Because You Are Beans

Because I love you,
I will plant a row of beans
In the Spring,
In May's Royal Belly.

I will water their hearts
And listen to their pulse,
I will feel their bodies
And touch fragile moments
Around their beds of earth,

I will tell them stories
Of Apollo at dusk
And Varuna at dawn.

Because I love you,
I will bring you to the garden
When their voices sing,
And You will grow
Beyond death.

Patrick T. Randolph

Borrowing My Wife's Soul

after William Carlos Williams

I have borrowed
your soul
that was in your
body

And which
you were probably
saving
for our love tonight.

Forgive me,
it felt so delightful
in which to soak—
so infinite
and
so you!

An Apple on the Kitchen Table

An apple on the kitchen table—
The smell of an orchard in late Autumn:

Sweet red globes bouncing in the air,
Rotating, stopping and then turning
In opposite motion.

I pick the apple up and inhale
Its small universe.

I bite into its crisp white center and let
The sweet, sticky juices drip
Down my fingers, hand and wrist.

An apple was on the kitchen table—
The late October sun
Reflecting off its red skin
In the warmth of Autumn's afternoon glow.

Patrick T. Randolph

Consequence of Love

Waking up
after
10,000 years
of one moment's sleep—

                    Your voice's light
                    has become the vision
                    of my eyes!

Just Up the Road—Early May

for Kelly

The Moon crawls across
Raindrops on a maple leaf.

Somewhere, just up the road,
Children are laughing at their father
Who makes funny faces while
Telling them stories—

Before their yawning eyes
Crawl across sleep to a dream.

The Quilter Creating

Each stitch she makes, her husband becomes warm;
Her eyes focus on color and create.
Months ago she examined each shape's form,
Deciding patterns like a magistrate.
She cut out the small triangles and squares,
Sewing them together, making a home
Of fabric where the home's creator cares.
When the sewing's done, her work is a dome
Draped over her knees and quilting begins.
Hands compose stitches, her aged fingers sing
While late Spring's calm afternoon light rescinds,
And darkness whispers to her eyes to bring
Her work to a close and offer a kiss
To her love whose face looks on in awed bliss.

Sleep

Silent music
        is the baby next door—
She wakes up
        and cries me to sleep.

Patrick T. Randolph

Weeding the Salad Garden

I share the early Spring garden
With a few robins and a couple black birds.

The black birds sing,
The robins hunt for worms,
And I weed the salad garden
Then work my way to the asparagus patch.

When I uproot an earthworm,
I give it a wink
And pack it back in the soil
Like a gift not to be seen
Until Christmas.

A robin looks at me—
A small piercing glance;

And I whistle
With a tone of guilt she easily reads
Like the largest letters
On an eye chart.

July 21

Mother's Birthday—

This is the hour
My grin's naturally

Mysterious
Sea pearl white light

Was first
                born!

Patrick T. Randolph

If Silence

million year
a woman

If Silence could speak
In silence, and
We could hear
Her loud and clear—
So quietly clear,

What would be
The first word
To leave Her lips—
Conveying the amazing
Beauty of Her heart?

Snowflake Philosophy

Every snowflake realizes
This is it.
It will never return to Earth
Again, at least not in its present
Form as Linda or Theo or Bob.

If it returns, its weight,
Size, shape, unique qualities,
Special powers, insights
And name will all be different.

Yes, this is it.

And that is why every snowflake
Including Linda, Theo or Bob

Falls to Earth in perfect precision—
Navigating its way and watching
Every existing thing around its tiny
Limitless reality.

They partake of Wind songs,
Moments of Sun, voices of Rain,

Every and any imaginable sound,
Trying to experience all;

And, if they're lucky,
They will land on the coat,
Hat, scarf, head or nose
Of their longed-after
Soulmate on Earth.

Patrick T. Randolph

Language of the Soil

My Spring toes, eyes, and nose were the first to learn
The language of the soil:

The difference in how it speaks
Using texture, color, and fragrance.

The words of the soft, potent, sour, black earth
Sing its language

Like a newly hatched bird who has just discovered
Its own ability to make sound.

Yes! And now, now

My Summer toes, eyes, and nose
Are equally excited by the phenomenon
Of communicating
With this solid, nurturing, soil companion,
With this solid, growing-everything grin,
With this guardian voice
Offering a place for life

To be born in a continual song
Of green growing greener

Inside the language, the giving, the Mothering
Of this selfless, sweet black soil.

My Wife's Hum

It starts with setting the breakfast table,
Her voice is still before creating sound.
First there is the whisper dark as sable,
Then the breath of dawn's light dancing around.
She looks out the clear morning windowpane,
Her fingers touch the curtain with a glance.
Her heartbeats grow without the smallest wane,
My wife's voice now begins to take a stance;
It runs through her causing love to appear
While her wise lips smile making my ears grin.
Ah, the sweet morning sound is coming near!
Its birth is small as the head of a pin.
But once her hum has finally begun
All things come running including the Sun!

My Nose Considering Your Nose

My nose is now considering your nose,
The first touch is cold like a greeting from a raindrop's mouth.

Our noses touch, and this kiss creates a tickling song from our
    lips
While our noses begin to entertain a love

Growing inside our eyes, lips, ears, tongues
And, of course, our noses' hearts.

My nose, on this late night bus, is now considering your nose,
Becoming excited by the possibility of our meeting in a few
    short hours.

My nose is in love with your nose,
Knowing nothing but the miracle of smell and the fact of this
    love for your nose.

Deer Lake Reflection

Pure starlight
Speckled on the black lake—
Stillness sings.

The smallest
Lapping of tiny ripples on
The shoreline;

Sky reflection
Bridges the Earth
With endless space.

Nothing on this
Night of simple miracles
Could erase

This pen-less poetry
Creating itself in perfect
Rhythmic verse.

A cricket joins
The night's celebration,
Then stops to

Disappear inside
The dark endless harmony
Of silent songs.

Patrick T. Randolph

A Wind God

for Mom and Dad

Empty robin's nest
Full of early Spring snowflakes—
Small whisper-touched hush;

A curious Wind appears—
Lifting snowflakes up—like birds.

Mother's Song

My mother's voice brings
The eyes of my ears back home
To see life's magic

And listen to her create
Orchards of grins in my lips.

Patrick T. Randolph

The Touch

for Ayfer and Haluk

Just for a moment,
On a cold car ferry boat
Leaving from the port—

His large hand on her shoulder,
She answers—eyes soaked with soul.

Sundays with Favre

"Rage, rage against the dying of the light."
—*Dylan Thomas*

Before the game starts, Favre grins at the crowd,
Letting fans know that all's right with the world.
This, oh, this is the time of religious
Awakenings and rebirth for all true
Midwestern folk—their fun-loving prophet
Will soon speak in the form of mystical
Throws through giant devilish defenders,
Audibles of quick intellect, scrambling
Movements of breathtaking poetry, pure
Sacred verse felt in the stadium and
Through the strange magic of the TV screen!
In the Midwest, our Bible is the ball—
Passed from one enlightened mind to another,
And our prophet is the blessed Brett Favre!
If it's third and thirteen, no need to fear,
Numbers are of no consequence with Brett,
He'll lead us out of temptation and save
Our souls with a quick slant pass to Shiancoe
Or send Rice deep to the end zone for a
Hail Mary—Oh yes! Another touchdown psalm!
Sundays with Favre are Sundays of pure light.
Even non-football fans stop to watch Brett
Create a moment of magical bliss—
A mystical reunion with his arm
Waving here and there—finding a safe home
For the Vikings' ball—a rebirth for all.
Such are Sundays with Favre, our purple god.
He is, no doubt, our messenger of truth,
So get on your knees, pray for the next win,
Close your eyes, and you'll see our prophet's grin!

101

Patrick T. Randolph

My Wife Returning from Turkey

for Gamze

I wake up, pull a grin out from inside
My soul's collection of elated masks,
I awake and let the grin slip with ease
Into my waiting lips! I rub my eyes,
And toss back the blue August bed covers!
I breathe and bounce my head off the white clouds,
I bounce my mind off the planet's laughter!
I whistle and let my spirit dance with
Strange uncontrolled blissful euphoria!
I grow songs and let my new body waltz
Through the small halls of our enchanted home—
Allowing all life to embrace my heart's
Amazingly energized desire to
Breathe and beat like a brand new Christmas drum!
I wash my face, I twirl into my clothes,
Slip into my shoes, and bolt out the door!
I celebrate life this day because you
Are returning to town today and all
The sky is sky and all the earth is earth,
And I am me waiting to rest my eyes
On you and the world altering moment
You appear from inside that airport bus!

Dusk on the Ridge

A wolf's ears
       balancing
              an April Moon.

Patrick T. Randolph

Silhouette

Scarecrow's arms,
Hands outstretched—
Holding Full Moon!

About the Poet and His Wife

Gamze and Patrick T. Randolph live in the green hills of southern Illinois. Gamze is originally from Istanbul, Turkey, the mystical city which fuses a kaleidoscope of humanity brimming with endless poetry. Her interests include crafts, film, art, traveling, and caring for her Turkish and American families. Patrick grew up on a small lake in the white birch, green pinewoods of Northwestern Wisconsin. Son of an English professor-farmer and a waitress-philosopher, he was born in River Falls, Wisconsin in 1967. Patrick teaches at the Center for English as a Second Language at Southern Illinois University Carbondale. He has had poems published in *Bellowing Ark, Byline Magazine, California Quarterly, Free Verse, Istanbul Literary Review, The Rockford Review, The Wisconsin Poets' Calendar* and many other journals in both the States and abroad. This is his first collection of poems.

About Popcorn Press

Popcorn Press is a micropublishing house based in southern Wisconsin, devoted to publishing fiction and poetry that is both genuine and unique.

Visit us online at www.PopcornPress.com.

Made in the USA
Lexington, KY
13 January 2017